50 delicious meals

Simple to prepare, quick to cook

SIMON HOLST

Published by Hyndman Publishing
325 Purchas Road, PO Box 19,
Amberly, RD2, Amberley,
North Canterbury

ISBN: 1-877168-78-5

© TEXT: Simon Holst

DESIGN: Dileva Design Ltd.

PHOTOGRAPHY: Lindsay Keats

HOME ECONOMISTS: Simon Holst and Alison Holst

All rights reserved. No part of this publication may be reproduced, stored in a retrieval system, or transmitted in any form, or by means electronic, photocopying, recording or otherwise without prior permission of the publisher in writing.

The recipes in this book have been carefully tested by the author. The publisher and the author have made every effort to ensure that the instructions are accurate and safe, but they cannot accept liability for any resulting injury or loss or damage to property, whether direct or consequential.

Because ovens and microwave ovens vary so much, you should take the cooking times suggested in recipes as guides only. The first time you make a recipe, check it at intervals to make sure it is not cooking faster, or more slowly than expected.

Always follow the detailed instructions given by manufacturers of your appliances and equipment, rather than the more general instructions given in these recipes.

Important Information:

For best results, use a standard metric (250ml) measuring cup and metric measuring spoons when you use these recipes.

1 tablespoon holds 15ml.
1 teaspoon holds 5ml.

All the cup and spoon measures in the recipes are level, unless otherwise stated. Sets of measuring cups make it easier to measure ¼ and ½ cup quantities.

Larger amounts of butter are given by weight. Use pack markings as a guide. Small amounts of butter are measured using spoons (1 tablespoon of butter weighs about 15 grams).

Abbreviations used:

ml	millilitre
tsp	teaspoon
Tbsp	tablespoon
g	gram
°C	Celsius
cm	centimetre

Acknowledgements:

I would like to thank the following firms:

- **Alison's Choice**: for the high quality dried fruit, fruit mixtures, crystallised fruit, nuts and seeds used in all recipe development and photographs.

- **Benniks Poultry Farm**, Buller Road, Levin, for RSPCA approved barn-laid eggs.

- **William Aitken**: for Lupi oils, grapeseed oil, and Balsamic vinegar.

Visit **www.hyndman.co.nz** or **www.holst.co.nz** for more information on other titles by this author.

COVER PHOTOGRAPH: Pasta with Pistachio & Parsley Pesto, page 10.

Introduction

Pasta, rice and noodles are incredibly popular, and it's easy to see why. They are inexpensive (at least in their basic forms), cook quickly, and keep well, so by stocking your pantry with a selection of a few varieties of each you can be sure you always have the basis for a number of easy meals on hand.

Another great feature of pasta, rice and noodles is the diversity of dishes that can be made from such simple ingredients. Pasta, rather obviously, tends to lend itself to Italian and/or Mediterranean dishes, while noodles form the basis for a huge variety of Asian dishes, from delicious soups to quick and easy stir-fries. Rice is used around the world, so you can choose from traditional European-style dishes such as risotto and paella through to Indian treats like biryani right through to South East Asian specialities like sushi or nasi goreng. The possibilities are virtually endless.

This is a collection of my favourite pasta, rice and noodle recipes. Most fall into the "but what am I going to make for dinner tonight?" category – that is, they can easily be made from scratch once you arrive home from work. Some of the others may require a little more time and effort, and are perfect to share with friends when entertaining…

Whatever the occasion, I'm sure you'll find something of interest here.

Happy cooking!

Simon Holst

Contents

Introduction	3
Pasta, Rice & Noodles – The Basics	4
Pasta	6
Pasta soups	6
Pasta salads	10
Pasta sauces	12
Baked pasta	23
Rice	**30**
Cool rice	30
Fried rice	34
Risottos & paella	40
Noodles	**46**
Noodle salads	46
Noodle soups	52
Stir-fried noodles	57
Index	**63**

Pasta, Rice and Noodles – The Basics

While I've tried to give some basic information in the individual recipes, there is seldom space to go into details about shapes, types or varieties, or cooking methods so here is a basic run down.

PASTA

The long and the short of choosing shapes: While some pasta dishes are traditionally made with particular pasta shapes, there are no hard and fast rules governing usage. Some dishes do lend themselves to long pasta (spaghetti, fettuccine etc.) and others to short shapes (macaroni, penne, spirals etc.), but they can be swapped around depending on your preferences (or what you have on hand!) Essentially the more complex the shape (more twists, ridges etc.), the greater the surface area and the more sauce it will hold.

Cooking Dried Pasta: There is no one "right" way, but these are my suggestions:

- Use a large pot and 2–3 cups of water per 100g of dried pasta. Salting the water is optional, but about ½ tsp salt per litre of water adds to the flavour a little.
- Have the water boiling rapidly before adding the pasta – the faster the water returns to the boil after the pasta is added, the firmer the cooked pasta will be and the less it will stick together.
- Leaving the pot uncovered (or partially covered) will help prevent boiling over (but does tend to steam up the kitchen).
- Use cooking time suggested on the packet as a guide, but start testing to see if it is "done" sooner rather than later – as soon as there is a hard core in the middle the pasta is cooked.
- Drain cooked pasta immediately, but don't shake out every last drop of water. Return cooked pasta to the cooking pot and toss it with about 1 Tbsp oil per 400–500g uncooked pasta, this gives a nice slippery coating and helps prevent sticking together.
- Add the sauce at the last minute before serving (unless specified otherwise in the recipe). Sauces and pasta can often be prepared in advance and reheated when required, but for best flavour and texture don't combine the two until just before serving.

Cooking Fresh Pasta: Most of the above also applies to cooking fresh pasta, but remember that cooking times for fresh pasta are usually much shorter – start testing after about 2–3 minutes. Fresh pasta is also more prone to foaming up and boiling over – it's best cooked uncovered and watched carefully.

RICE

There are many different types of rice on the market. Essentially they fall into two categories, short grain (arborio, sushi) which absorb more liquid as they cook and have a softer texture and medium-long grain (calrose, jasmine, basmati) which are good steamed or boiled. I always keep at least two varieties on hand, arborio for risottos and paella, and jasmine or basmati (fragrant varieties which have a little more flavour than 'plain' varieties) that I use for pretty much everything else.

Cooking Medium-Long Grain White Rice: There are many, many different ways to cook rice, but these are the methods I find most successful. (Allow 1 cup of rice for 3–4 servings.)

MICROWAVING: place 1 cup of rice in a large microwave bowl, add ¼–½ tsp salt and 2–2¼ cups of boiling water, then cover and cook at Medium (50%) power for 15 minutes or until tender.

BOILING: bring 8 cups of water plus 2 tsp salt to a rapid boil in a large pot. Sprinkle in 1 cup of rice then boil gently for 10–12 minutes until grains are tender through. Drain in a large sieve and rinse with hot water if sticky.

Brown Rice (and blends): Brown rice is high in fibre and has an interesting nutty flavour; the down side is it takes longer to cook. Microwave as above adding an extra ¼ cup boiling water and increasing the cooking time to 25–30 minutes, or boil for about 20–25 minutes until tender.

NOODLES

Noodles and pasta are really very similar – if you can't find the noodles specified in a recipe (although most supermarkets carry a reasonable range) you can usually substitute spaghetti or vermicelli instead.

Cooking Noodles: Most of the pasta pointers also apply to Asian noodles, but there are some exceptions.

- Dried noodles often seem to contain more salt, don't salt the water unless you like particularly salty food.

- Noodles are often thinner and require shorter cooking times.

- Fresh (and vacuum packed) yellow egg noodles, fresh fine egg noodles and udon (and fresh rice noodles, if you can get them) need very little cooking. A brief rinse with boiling water, or light steaming is often all that is required.

- Rice noodles (or rice sticks) and bean thread (cellophane or glass) noodles do not require cooking as such – a soak in boiling water is all that is required. Place them in a large container, cover with boiling water and leave to soak until they are tender through (3–10 minutes depending on thickness).

- Rice and bean thread vermicelli can also be fried (they puff up into crunchy and delicious threads) straight from dry.

Pasta

Minestrone

While the ingredients list does look long, this delicious soup is really quite simple to make and is substantial enough to form the basis of a meal.

For 6–8 servings:
1 Tbsp olive oil
1–2 rashers bacon (optional)
2 cloves garlic
1 large onion, diced
4 cups chicken or vegetable stock
2 medium carrots
2 medium sticks celery
1 medium potato
425g can kidney beans
400g can whole tomatoes in juice
¾ cup small pasta shapes
1 cup frozen peas
2 cups sliced cabbage
2 Tbsp chopped parsley
2 Tbsp pesto or ¼ cup chopped basil (optional)
½ tsp each dried oregano and thyme
1 tsp salt
freshly ground black pepper
grated Parmesan cheese and pesto to serve

Heat the oil in a large pot over a medium heat. Chop the bacon (if using) and cook until golden, then add the chopped garlic and onion. Cook, stirring occasionally, for 5 minutes or until the onion is soft and clear.

Stir in stock, then add the finely diced fresh vegetables. Add the drained and rinsed beans, then the canned tomatoes, breaking them up with a fork. Bring the soup to the boil, then reduce the heat, cover and simmer for 30 minutes or until the potato is tender.

Add the pasta, peas, cabbage, herbs and seasonings. Simmer for 10–15 minutes or until the pasta is tender but still firm. Check the seasoning and add some water if you think the soup is too thick.

Ladle into warm soup bowls, topping each serving with a little freshly grated Parmesan cheese and/or a spoonful of pesto.

NOTE: For vegetarian soup, omit the bacon and use vegetable rather than chicken stock.

Pasta & Bean Soup

This soup is not only delicious, it is substantial enough to serve as a meal and very quick to prepare, taking 15–20 minutes from start to finish.

For 4–6 servings:
3 Tbsp olive oil
1 clove of garlic, chopped
1 medium onion
50g cubed ham or bacon (optional)
½ tsp chilli powder
2 bay leaves
¼ tsp dried thyme
400g can diced tomatoes
425g can red kidney beans
440g can four bean mix
4 cups chicken stock
1 cup small pasta shapes
salt and pepper to taste
chopped fresh parsley or pesto and/or grated Parmesan to serve

Heat the oil in a large pot. Add the garlic and the sliced onion (plus ham or bacon if using) and cook, without browning, until the onion is soft and clear. Stir in the chilli, bay leaves and thyme, and cook for one minute longer.

Add the tomatoes, rinsed beans and the stock. Heat until boiling, then add the pasta. Allow to boil gently until the pasta is cooked (10–15 minutes), then add salt and pepper to taste.

Serve topped with some chopped fresh parsley or basil (or a little pesto) and some freshly shaved or grated Parmesan.

Basil Pesto

Pesto is incredibly versatile – it makes a delicious pasta sauce on its own, but can also transform many other dishes into something really special.

For 1–1½ cups:
4 cloves garlic
4 cups (150g) basil leaves
½ cup pine nuts
½ cup grated Parmesan cheese
½ –1 cup olive oil
salt to taste

Put the peeled garlic, basil and pine nuts into a food processor and process until well chopped. Add the Parmesan and half a cup of oil and process until well mixed. Start adding the extra olive oil a tablespoon at a time until you have a fairly smooth paste that just holds its shape.

Add salt to taste, then spoon into an airtight container for storage. Pour a little extra oil on top of the pesto to help prevent browning.

To use as a pasta sauce alone, simply toss pesto through freshly cooked, lightly oiled pasta (allow about ¼ of a cup of pesto per 100g uncooked pasta).

NOTE: Making pesto also provides an excellent way to keep fresh basil all year; just divide a large batch into small jars and freeze until required.

Pasta Niçoise

The flavours of this are based on the classic, salade niçoise, but with a twist, replacing the potatoes with pasta.

For 2–3 servings:
250g small pasta shells
2 eggs
150g fresh green beans
3–4 medium tomatoes
12–16 black olives
1–2 Tbsp capers
½ cup mayonnaise
2 Tbsp lemon juice
2 Tbsp olive oil
½ tsp salt
black pepper
210g can tuna (in oil or brine)
¼ cup chopped parsley

Put the pasta on to cook in plenty of boiling water. Prick the rounded ends of the egg shells (to prevent bursting) and add the eggs to the pasta water to hard-boil.

Boil or steam the beans until tender, cool them in cold water, then cut into 4–5cm lengths. Place these in a bowl, then add the cubed tomatoes, olives and capers. Add the mayonnaise, lemon juice, oil, salt and pepper and mix gently until well combined. Drain the tuna, and add to the vegetable mixture.

Drain the cooked pasta (removing the eggs), then add the tuna and vegetable mixture and the chopped parsley. Stir gently to combine. Transfer to a serving bowl (or bowls) and garnish with the quartered or roughly chopped hard-boiled eggs.

Serve warm or chilled, either alone or with crusty bread.

Pasta with Pistachio & Parsley Pesto ▸

Pistachios, parsley and avocado oil give this a vibrant green colour and nutty flavour.

For 4 servings:
1 cup (100g) unshelled pistachios
400g packet fresh pasta
1 cup (60g) parsley
2 cloves garlic
½ cup avocado oil
½ tsp salt
extra avocado oil

Shell the pistachios (this yields about ½ cup). Boil the pasta according to packet instructions. While it cooks, put the parsley, garlic, and oil in a food processor and blend until finely chopped. Add the nuts and salt and process until nuts are finely chopped. (Add more oil if mixture seems too dry.)

Toss the pesto through the drained pasta, adding a little extra oil if desired. Serve topped with shavings of Parmesan and a few extra chopped pistachios.

NOTE: This pesto is also delicious mixed with oil and brushed over bread to make crostini, or try it spooned over grilled chicken or fried fish.

Pasta Primavera

This quick and easy dish can be made any time of year, but always seems particularly good in spring made with delicious new season's vegetables.

For 4 servings:
2 cups fresh vegetables
   (asparagus, baby carrots,
   mange tout or snow peas,
   broad beans, scallopini or
   zucchini, broccoli florets etc.)
400g fresh fettuccine
¾–1 cup cream
¼ cup dry white wine
½ cup grated Parmesan
¼ cup chopped basil or
   1–2 Tbsp pesto
salt and pepper to taste
1–2 Tbsp olive oil
extra Parmesan and/or chopped
   basil to serve

Fresh pasta cooks very quickly, so prepare the vegetables before you start cooking. Cut asparagus spears into 4–5cm lengths and other selected vegetables into similar sized pieces.

Bring a large pot of lightly salted water to a rapid boil, then add the pasta. Place the vegetables, slower cooking ones first (carrots, broccoli etc.), in a sieve or steamer over the pasta and cook until just tender.

Heat the cream and wine in another pot or pan, bring to the boil and reduce down a little. Remove from the heat and stir in the Parmesan and basil or pesto. Season to taste with salt and pepper.

Drain the vegetables and pasta, add the olive oil and toss to coat. Add the sauce then stir gently or toss again.

Top with some additional Parmesan and/or basil and serve immediately, accompanied with some good, crusty bread or rolls.

Penne with Broccoli, Mushroom & Almonds

This is a really simple, but nonetheless very good sauce.

For 2–3 servings:
200–300g penne
½ cup slivered almonds
2 Tbsp olive oil
2 cloves garlic
100g mushrooms, sliced
1 head broccoli (350–400g), cut
   into small florets
½ cup cream
1 Tbsp pesto
50g creamy blue cheese, cubed
salt and pepper to taste

Put the pasta on to cook in plenty of boiling water. While the pasta cooks, prepare the sauce. First heat a large pan and toast the slivered almonds until they are golden, then remove and set aside.

Heat the oil in the same pan, then add the garlic and cook for about a minute. Stir in the mushrooms and broccoli florets and stir-fry until the mushrooms are soft and the broccoli is tender.

Add the cream, pesto, and the cubed blue cheese. Stir until well combined and the blue cheese has melted. Taste, and add salt and pepper as required, then remove the sauce from the heat.

Drain the cooked pasta, and toss it with a little extra olive oil or butter. Add the sauce and the toasted slivered almonds, stir gently until well combined, and serve.

30 Minute Bolognese

This sauce may not be all that close to the original Italian version, but it is still very good.

For 4–6 servings:
2 Tbsp olive oil
1 medium onion, diced
2 cloves garlic, chopped
1 medium carrot, finely diced
1 stick celery, thinly sliced
400–500g lean minced beef
½ tsp dried basil
½ tsp dried marjoram
400g can whole or diced tomatoes in juice
300g can tomato purée
½–1 tsp salt
black pepper to taste
400–500g spaghetti or fettuccine, etc.
1–2 Tbsp olive oil or butter

Heat the oil in a large pan. Add the onion and garlic and cook for 2–3 minutes, stirring frequently, until the onion is soft.

Stir in the carrot and celery and cook for a minute longer, then add the beef. Cook, stirring frequently, until the beef has lost its pink colour. Add the herbs, tomatoes and tomato purée.

Allow the mixture to boil, then reduce the heat to a gentle simmer and cover with a lid. Simmer gently, for 10–15 minutes, stirring occasionally, while you cook the pasta (if the sauce begins to look dry add a ¼ cup pasta water or wine).

Drain the cooked pasta and toss it with the oil or butter then arrange on individual plates or a platter. Spoon the sauce over the pasta and top with some chopped parsley and/or grated Parmesan. Serve accompanied by a salad or vegetables and crusty bread.

Macaroni Cheese

This is my ultimate comfort food!

For 4–6 servings:
400–500g macaroni or spirals
3 Tbsp butter
3 Tbsp flour
¼ tsp grated nutmeg
½ tsp salt
2 cups milk
1 tsp mild mustard (optional)
2 cups (200g) grated cheese, either cheddar, Gruyere or half and half

Optional Topping: ½–1 cup grated cheese, preferably Gruyere, or ½ cup fresh bread crumbs mixed with 2 Tbsp melted butter.

Put the pasta on to cook in plenty of boiling water. While the pasta cooks, melt the butter in a medium-sized pot. Stir in the flour and cook for 2–3 minutes, stirring continuously to avoid browning. Add the nutmeg and salt, then begin adding the milk half a cup at a time. Stir briskly to break up any lumps and allow the sauce to thicken and boil between each addition. When all the milk has been added and the sauce has returned to the boil, remove it from the heat.

Add the mustard and the grated cheese, stirring until the cheese has melted and the sauce is smooth and creamy.

Drain the cooked pasta and stir in sauce. Serve as is or transfer to an oven-proof dish and top with the additional grated cheese or bread crumb mixture. Place under a preheated grill until the top bubbles and/or turns golden brown. Serve and enjoy!

Spaghetti & Mussels

Mussels, wine, garlic, tomatoes and basil combine to make a beautiful and delicious topping for spaghetti or other long pasta.

For 2–3 servings:
2 cloves garlic, chopped
1 cup dry white wine
½ tsp dried basil
black pepper, to taste
1kg live mussels
400g can whole or diced tomatoes in juice
1 Tbsp tomato paste
1–2 Tbsp chopped basil (optional)
300–400g fresh spaghetti
1–2 Tbsp olive oil

Place the garlic, wine, dried basil, and black pepper in a large pan or pot with a close-fitting lid, and heat to boiling.

Add the mussels to the pot, then cover tightly and steam for 3–4 minutes. Remove the opened mussels, then re-cover the remaining mussels and steam for another 2–3 minutes. Collect the opened mussels and discard any that have still not opened.

Add the tomatoes, tomato paste and half of the fresh basil (if using) to the wine-mussel liquid and leave to simmer over a medium heat, stirring occasionally.

Cook the pasta in plenty of boiling water while the sauce reduces and thickens. Drain the cooked pasta and toss it with a little olive oil. Arrange the cooked pasta in individual bowls or on a serving platter, and arrange the steamed mussels on top of this. Pour over the sauce and top with the remaining chopped basil. Serve immediately, accompanied with a crisp green salad and bread. (Don't forget to give people a dish for the mussel shells.)

Spaghetti Puttanesca

This bold and spicy sauce is quick and easy to prepare from a few ingredients that can be kept on hand in the fridge and pantry.

For 3–4 servings:
2 Tbsp olive oil
2–3 anchovy fillets, chopped
1 medium onion, sliced
2 cloves garlic, chopped
½–1 tsp chilli powder
½ tsp each basil and oregano
400g can whole or diced tomatoes in juice
15–20 black olives
1 Tbsp capers, chopped
¼ cup dry red wine
salt and pepper to taste
300–400g spaghetti
grated Parmesan to serve

Heat the oil in a large pan. Add the anchovy and cook, stirring frequently, until the pieces break up. Add the onion and the garlic to the pan. Cook until the onion has softened and is beginning to turn clear.

Stir in the chilli, herbs, and tomatoes in juice (break up whole tomatoes, if required). Bring to the boil and then add the olives, capers and wine, then season to taste with salt and pepper. Reduce the heat and leave to simmer while you cook the pasta.

Toss a little additional olive oil through the cooked pasta, then top the spaghetti with the sauce and a little chopped fresh parsley. Serve immediately, accompanied with a bowl of freshly grated Parmesan cheese and a bottle of red wine!

Bacon & Mushroom Sauce

Another really delicious sauce that can easily be prepared while the pasta cooks.

For 3 large servings:
250–300g short pasta (spirals, penne etc.)
150g bacon
2 Tbsp olive oil
1 medium onion, diced
150g mushrooms, sliced
½ tsp dried sage
½ tsp dried thyme
½ tsp salt
black pepper
¼ cup vegetable stock or white wine
½ cup cream
chopped parsley and/or grated Parmesan to serve

Put the pasta on to cook in plenty of lightly salted boiling water. While the pasta cooks prepare the sauce.

Cut the bacon crossways into 1cm strips. Heat the oil in a large pan, then cook the bacon until it is brown and turning crispy. Remove bacon from the pan and drain on paper towels. Pour any excess fat from the pan (leaving about 2 tablespoons) and add the diced onion. Sauté until the onion is soft and clear, add the sliced mushrooms and cook, stirring frequently, until these begin to soften.

Add the seasonings and the stock or wine. Simmer over a moderate heat for 2 minutes, then add the cream and bacon. Increase the heat so the sauce is boiling vigorously and cook for another 2 minutes, stirring frequently, to allow the sauce to reduce down and thicken a little.

Drain the pasta as soon as it is cooked, then return it to the pot and add the sauce. Stir to mix thoroughly.

Leave to stand for one to two minutes, then serve topped with some chopped fresh parsley and/or freshly grated Parmesan.

Fettuccine with Ham & Peas

This simple and delicious dish can't be called low fat, but it makes a great occasional treat.

For 3–4 servings:
1 tsp olive oil
50g butter
200g ham
1 Tbsp flour
300ml cream
¼ cup white wine or milk
1 cup frozen peas
1 Tbsp basil pesto
½ tsp salt
black pepper to taste
400g fettuccine
extra olive oil or butter

Put on a large pot of water for the pasta. While the water comes to the boil, heat the oil and butter in a large frypan. Cut the ham into matchsticks, then add them to the pan and sauté, stirring frequently, until golden brown. Stir in the flour and cook for a minute longer. Pour in the cream and wine or milk and allow the mixture to come to the boil before adding the peas, pesto and seasonings. Reduce the heat to very low (or turn off the element but don't remove the pan) and leave to simmer gently while you cook the pasta.

Drain the cooked pasta and toss with a little olive oil (or additional butter), before gently stirring through the sauce. Serve immediately, topped with a generous grind of pepper and/or some chopped basil and/or grated Parmesan.

Bacon & Egg Pasta

Eggs, milk (or cream) and a little cheese make a delicious and unbelievably simple pasta sauce.

For 3–4 servings:
250–300g short pasta
1 Tbsp oil
150–200g bacon, cut in 5mm strips
2–3 spring onions
2 large eggs
½ cup milk or cream
salt and pepper to taste
2 Tbsp butter
½ cup grated cheese
½ cup peas or diced tomato (optional)

Put the pasta on to cook in plenty of lightly salted boiling water. While it cooks, heat the oil in a large frypan. Add the bacon and cook for 3–4 minutes, stirring occasionally until it begins to brown. Stir in the spring onions (if using) and cook for 2–3 minutes longer, then remove from the heat.

Break the eggs into a small bowl and add the milk or cream and salt and pepper to taste. Whisk with a fork until well combined.

Drain the cooked pasta and return it to the cooking pot. Add the butter, bacon (and any drippings), cheese, and vegetables (if using), and then pour in the egg mixture. Stir gently over a very low heat until the sauce thickens, usually about 2–3 minutes. Serve with your favourite salad or cooked vegetables.

Easy Spaghetti & Meatballs

Baking meatballs instead of browning them in a pan saves time and effort – you can cook the pasta and make the sauce while the meatballs are in the oven.

For 4 servings:
2–3 thick slices of bread
1 small onion
1 clove garlic, peeled
500g lean minced beef
1 egg
½ tsp each basil, oregano, thyme and chilli powder
1 tsp salt
400g fresh or dried spaghetti
1 Tbsp olive oil
2 cloves garlic, chopped
2 x 400g cans whole or diced tomatoes in juice
½ tsp each basil and oregano
½ cup red or white wine
salt and pepper to taste
grated Parmesan and/or chopped basil or parsley to serve

Turn on the oven to 220°C. Break the bread into smaller pieces and chop finely in a food processor. Add the quartered onion and garlic, and chop finely. Add the next seven ingredients and mix in bursts, just until everything is combined. Divide the mixture in quarters, then eighths, then sixteenths, and then into 32 portions, shaping them into balls with wet hands.

Arrange the meatballs in a single layer in an uncovered baking pan lined with Teflon or baking paper and bake for 12–15 minutes, or until a halved meatball is no longer pink in the middle.

While meatballs bake, cook the spaghetti in plenty of lightly salted boiling water, and prepare the sauce.

Heat the oil in a large pan and cook the garlic for about 1 minute. Add the tomatoes (with the juice) to the pan, forcing the solids through a large sieve with the back of a spoon (discard the seeds and any tough bits that remain). Add the wine and seasonings, and allow the sauce to simmer gently for about 5 minutes. The sauce doesn't need to be too thick; just thick enough to coat the meatballs.

Drain the cooked pasta, return it to the cooking pot, and toss it with 1–2 Tbsp butter. Either add the meatballs to the pan with the sauce, toss to coat and spoon over the pasta, or spoon the sauce over the pasta, then top with the meatballs. A sprinkling of grated Parmesan and/or some chopped parsley or basil makes a nice finishing touch.

Basic Beef Lasagne

For many of the younger generation, beef lasagne is now well and truly entrenched as a comfort food. I can relate to this – it is hard to beat.

For 4–6 servings:
2 Tbsp olive oil
2 medium onions, diced
1 green pepper, diced
750g lean minced beef
400g can whole or diced
    tomatoes in juice
2 Tbsp tomato paste
½ tsp each thyme and oregano
1 tsp each basil and salt
black pepper to taste
2 Tbsp butter
3 Tbsp flour
½ tsp salt
¼ tsp grated nutmeg
2 cups milk
1 cup grated tasty cheese
about 250g lasagne sheets
2 Tbsp grated Parmesan
a little paprika

Heat the oil in a large pan. Add the onions and cook until softened. Stir in the pepper and cook for one to two minutes longer. Tip in the beef and cook, stirring to break up any lumps, until the meat has lost its pink colour. Add the tomatoes (break up whole tomatoes if required), and the tomato paste and seasonings. Continue to cook, stirring occasionally for another five minutes while you prepare the cheese sauce.

Melt the butter in a medium-sized pot. As soon as the butter is melted stir in the flour and cook for 2–3 minutes, stirring continuously to avoid browning. Add the salt, then the grated nutmeg, and begin adding the milk half a cup at a time. Stir briskly to break up any lumps, and allow the sauce to thicken and boil between each addition. When all the milk has been added and the sauce has thickened, remove the sauce from the heat and stir in the grated cheese.

To assemble the lasagne, lightly oil a shallow (5cm) casserole or lasagne dish (about 20x30cm). Spread a quarter of the beef mixture over the bottom and cover this with a layer of lasagne. Repeat this process so you finish with four layers of each, and finish with a layer of lasagne. Pour the cheese sauce over the top and sprinkle this with the grated Parmesan and a little paprika.

Bake at 175°C for 40 minutes. Serve with salad/s of your choice and plain or garlic bread.

Spinach & Mushroom Lasagne

This long time favourite is always popular and, for lasagne, is relatively straightforward.

For 4–6 servings:
2 Tbsp olive or canola oil
2 cloves garlic, chopped
1 medium onion, diced
250g mushrooms, sliced
½ tsp each dried thyme and marjoram
500g frozen spinach, thawed
1 cup cottage cheese
½ tsp salt
2–3 Tbsp butter
¼ cup flour
2 cups milk
salt and pepper to taste
½ tsp freshly grated nutmeg
1 cup grated cheese
250–300g curly lasagne or sheets
paprika

Preheat the oven to 170°C. Meanwhile heat the oil in a large pan. Add garlic and onion and cook until onion is soft, then add the mushrooms and herbs. Cook for two to three minutes longer, then set aside. Combine the spinach, cottage cheese and salt in a bowl.

Melt butter in a medium-sized pot. Add the flour and cook, stirring continuously, for about a minute. Pour in a third of the milk and bring to the boil, stirring vigorously to ensure there are no lumps. Allow sauce to boil, then stir in half the remaining milk and boil again. Stir in remaining milk and boil once again. Remove from the heat and add the seasonings and grated cheese, stirring until cheese melts.

Non-stick spray a 20x30cm lasagne dish. Cover the bottom with a single layer of lasagne. Spread half of the spinach mixture evenly over the lasagne. Arrange another layer of lasagne over the spinach and cover with the mushroom mixture. Add another layer of lasagne, then the remaining spinach and a final layer of lasagne. Pour the sauce over the top and dust with paprika.

Bake for 40–45 minutes. Serve with bread and/or a side salad.

Smoked Salmon & Mushroom Lasagne

This super easy and elegant dish makes a small quantity of smoked salmon go a long way!

For 4 servings:
3 Tbsp butter
3 Tbsp flour
¼ tsp grated nutmeg
2½ cups milk
2 cups grated cheese
salt and pepper to taste
200g mushrooms, sliced
150–200g smoked salmon, sliced
100–200g fresh lasagne

Preheat the oven to 170°C. Melt the butter in a medium-sized pot. As soon as the butter is melted stir in the flour and cook for about 2 minutes, stirring continuously. Add the nutmeg, then begin adding the milk half a cup at a time. Stir briskly and allow the sauce to thicken and boil between each addition. When all the milk has been added and the sauce has thickened, remove the sauce from the heat and stir in about ¾ of the grated cheese.

Non-stick spray a shallow 20x25cm lasagne dish. Spread half the mushrooms and half the smoked salmon over the bottom of the dish. Cover these with a third of the sauce, then half of the lasagne. Make another layer with the remaining mushrooms and salmon, and half the remaining sauce. Cover this with the remaining lasagne and cover with the remaining sauce.

Sprinkle with the rest of the grated cheese, then cover loosely with foil and bake for 30 minutes. Uncover and bake for a further 15–20 minutes until the top is golden brown. Serve with a green or tomato salad and crusty bread or garlic bread.

NOTE: Lasagne can be made ahead and reheated, covered (about 30 minutes, or until the centre is warm, at 170°C), when required.

Alison's Lazy Lasagne

This is a variant of one of my mother's very popular recipes. It's almost too good to be true – lasagne with no precooking, and just a little assembly!

For 4–6 servings:
2 cloves garlic, chopped
400g can whole or diced tomatoes in juice
420g can tomato soup
500g minced beef
2 Tbsp tomato paste
1 tsp each basil and oregano
½ tsp salt
200g curly lasagne

Topping:
2 tsp cornflour
1 egg
¾ cup milk, sour cream, or a mixture
1 cup grated tasty cheese
paprika (optional)

Turn the oven on to heat to 180°C. While the oven heats, put the garlic and tomatoes (and juice) into a food processor or large bowl and process or mash with a fork to break up the tomatoes. Add the soup, minced beef, tomato paste, herbs and salt, and process or mix until well combined.

Non-stick spray or oil a 23cm square or a 25x20cm rectangular ovenware dish. Spread a third of the meat mixture evenly over the bottom. Place half the lasagne over the meat. Repeat the layering with another third of the meat mixture and the remaining lasagne, and then cover with the remaining meat mixture. (You may like to keep a bit more than a third of the meat mixture for the top layer.)

Place in the oven and bake for 50 minutes. Check after 30 minutes and cover with foil if looking dry.

Make the topping by mixing together the cornflour, egg, milk (and/or sour cream) and cheese. Pour this over the cooked mixture evenly, sprinkle with paprika, and bake, uncovered, at 150°C for about 10 minutes or until the topping sets.

Leave to stand 15–30 minutes before cutting into squares or rectangles. Serve immediately, or refrigerate. Cut into serving-sized pieces and wrap in cling film for freezing. Reheat in a moderate oven or microwave.

Serve with a green salad or cooked vegetables and garlic bread.

Salmon & Mushroom Cannelloni

Keep a large can of salmon and some cannelloni on hand in your pantry and you can knock this up to impress friends or family at relatively short notice!

For 4–6 servings:
2 Tbsp olive oil
1 medium onion, chopped
1 clove garlic, minced
200g small button mushrooms, sliced
415g can pink salmon
½ cup ricotta or cottage cheese
2–3 Tbsp chopped parsley
2 Tbsp capers (optional)
1 Tbsp chopped fresh dill (optional)
25g butter
¼ cup flour
2½ cups milk
salt and pepper to taste
¼ tsp freshly grated nutmeg
2 cups grated cheese
paprika
16–20 (about 200g) cannelloni tubes

Heat the oil in a large pan. Add the chopped onion and minced garlic and cook for about 2 minutes, stirring frequently. Stir in the sliced mushrooms (if the mushrooms are too large you may need to halve the slices) and cook for another two minutes. Open and drain the salmon, and add this along with the ricotta (or cottage cheese), capers and herbs. Stir until the filling ingredients are well combined, removing any obvious salmon bones. Set the filling aside to cool while you prepare the sauce.

Melt the butter in a medium-sized pot. Add the flour and stir well so there are no lumps. Cook, stirring continuously, for about a minute. Pour in a third of the milk and bring to the boil, stirring vigorously to ensure there are no lumps. Allow the sauce to thicken and boil for a minute, then add half the remaining milk and bring to the boil again, stirring frequently. Repeat using the last of the milk, then remove the sauce from the heat. Add the seasonings and 1 cup of grated cheese. Stir until the cheese melts.

Pour a third of the cheese sauce into an oiled casserole dish. (Check to see that it will hold the cannelloni before you start.) Stuff the filling into the cannelloni tubes using clean hands – there is no tidy way to do this! Arrange the filled cannelloni tubes in the dish. Pour over the remaining sauce, and sprinkle with the rest of the grated cheese and a few pinches of paprika.

Bake at 220°C for 30-40 minutes. Serve with crusty bread, a green or tomato salad, or steamed seasonal vegetables.

Rice

Sushi

A platter of several different shapes of sushi makes a tasty and interesting meal.

For 3–4 main servings:
2 cups short-grain rice
3 cups boiling water
3 Tbsp rice vinegar
3 Tbsp sugar
2 Tbsp sherry
2 tsp salt

Fillings:
strips of cucumber
strips of carrot
sliced avocado
strips of red/green/yellow
 capsicum
smoked (or raw) salmon
strips of omelette
shredded surimi
fresh (or canned) tuna
pickled ginger
pickled vegetables
wasabi paste
yaki nori (roasted seaweed
 sheets)

Place the rice in a large container and rinse twice with cold water. Put the rice in a large microwave bowl, add the boiling water then cover the bowl and microwave at Medium (50%) power for 15–20 minutes, until tender. Stir in the vinegar, sugar, sherry and salt then cool to room temperature.

To cook conventionally: Put rice in a large pot, add the boiling water, bring to the boil, then cover and reduce the heat to very low and steam for 15 minutes. Remove from the heat and stand for a further 10 minutes before stirring in the vinegar, sugar, sherry and salt.

◀ The fillings you choose will depend on the type of sushi you are making and your own preferences, but the list on the left has a few suggestions.

Rolled Sushi (Maki-sushi)

Lie a sheet of nori on a clean dry bench. Spread a layer of rice about 1cm thick over the nori, leaving a 2–3cm strip down one long edge clear. Arrange selected filling/s along the middle of the rice. Brush the exposed nori with a little water, then roll up starting from the rice-covered edge. Sit the roll seam side down for 2–3 minutes before cutting into 2–3cm thick slices.

Hand Rolls (Temaki-sushi)

Cut a sheet of nori in half lengthwise. Place one strip on the bench and spread a heaped tablespoon of rice diagonally across one end. Arrange selected fillings on top of the rice. Fold the exposed corner across the filling, then roll the sheet up to form a cone.

Moulded Sushi (Nigiri-sushi)

Squeeze and shape a heaped tablespoon of rice until it is flat on the bottom and curved on the top. Spread one side of a thin slice of raw (or cold smoked) salmon or tuna with wasabi, then place it wasabi side down over the curved side of the rice. Decorate with a thin 'belt' of nori if desired.

Sushi Rice Salad

This delicious salad contains all of my favourite sushi ingredients, but is easy to prepare because they are just tossed together!

For 2–3 main course servings:
1 cup medium-grain rice
2 cups boiling water
50–100g cold-smoked salmon (or 100–200g surimi)
pickled (pink) ginger, thinly sliced (optional)
2–3 sheets yaki nori (grilled seaweed sheets)
1 avocado, peeled and cubed
½ telegraph cucumber, cubed
1 medium carrot, finely diced

Dressing:
2 Tbsp sherry
2 Tbsp canola oil
1 Tbsp Kikkoman soy sauce
1 Tbsp rice wine or wine vinegar
1 Tbsp sugar
½ tsp salt
1–2 tsp wasabi paste (to taste)
1–2 tsp grated fresh ginger (optional)

Cover rice with the boiling water, then cover and microwave at Medium (50%) power for 15 minutes so the grains are completely tender. While the rice cooks, prepare the dressing by measuring all the ingredients into a screw-top jar then shaking until well blended.

When the rice is cooked, pour in half the dressing and stir until well combined. Leave the rice to stand until cool (refrigerate if preparing in advance).

Cut the salmon into strips about 1cm wide (or shred the surimi), and cut or tear the nori sheets into strips about 1cm wide and 4cm long.

Stir the avocado, cucumber and carrot into the rice, along with the salmon (or surimi), ginger, nori (reserve a little to garnish) and the remaining dressing. Toss to combine.

Garnish with the reserved nori strips and serve. Accompany with little bowls of extra soy sauce and wasabi if desired.

VARIATION: The soy sauce in the dressing gives the salad a good flavour, but does 'muddy' the colour a little. If you prefer, omit it from the dressing and serve it on the side – little dipping sauce bowls are excellent for this.

Chicken Fried Rice

My children love this dish, perhaps because of its simplicity. If you don't have a large pan or wok, make it in fairly small quantities.

For 2–3 servings:
250g boneless, skinless chicken breast or thighs
2 tsp soy sauce
1 tsp sesame oil
1 tsp grated ginger (optional)
2–3 Tbsp canola or other oil
1 large egg
1 Tbsp water
1–2 spring onions, finely chopped
1 medium carrot, grated
¼ cup frozen peas
1½–2 cups (preferably cool) cooked rice*
¼–½ tsp salt

Put the chicken in a plastic bag and add the soy sauce, sesame oil and ginger (if using), then massage the bag so the chicken is coated. Leave to marinate for 15 minutes (or refrigerate for up to 24 hours).

Heat 1 tsp of the oil in a large non-stick pan. Add the chicken and cook for 3–5 minutes per side, depending on thickness, until cooked through, then remove from the pan and set aside.

Lightly beat the egg and water together, then pour into the pan. Cook until it sets into a thin omelette, then lift out and set aside.

Add another tablespoon of oil to the pan. When it is hot add the spring onion and carrot and stir-fry for 2–3 minutes. Stir in the peas, rice and a further tablespoon of oil. Cook, stirring frequently, for another 3–4 minutes or until the rice is heated through. (Add a little extra oil if the rice is sticking.)

Slice or dice the chicken and the omelette and stir these into the mixture. Season to taste and serve.

*To cook the rice place ½ cup long-grain rice in a microwave bowl with 1 cup boiling water and a pinch of salt. Cover, then microwave for 15 minutes at Medium (50%) power. If necessary, spread cooked rice on a tray to cool quickly.

Nasi Goreng

Like most fried rice dishes, nasi goreng works best if you use cold cooked rice. One big advantage of this is that you can whip up a meal in minutes.

For 3–4 servings:
1 large onion, peeled and quartered
2 cloves garlic, crushed and peeled
1–2cm piece ginger, peeled
1 tsp minced red chilli (optional)
250g pork loin steaks, cut into 1cm cubes
4–6 spring onions, sliced, with white and green parts separated
2 Tbsp canola oil
2 large eggs, lightly beaten
1 medium carrot, finely diced
3 cups cold cooked rice*
2 Tbsp canola oil
200–250g cooked shrimp
2 Tbsp light soy sauce
1 tsp sugar
¼–½ cucumber, sliced, to garnish

Place the onion, garlic, ginger and chilli (if using) in a blender or food processor and process until they form a smooth paste. Stir the pork cubes into the paste and leave to stand for a few minutes while you prepare the remaining ingredients.

Thinly slice the white parts of the spring onions while the first measure of oil heats in a wok or large frypan. Add the sliced spring onions and cook, stirring occasionally, until golden brown (do not overcook as they will turn bitter). Remove from the pan and drain on paper towels. Tip the oil into a heatproof container and reserve.

Return the pan or wok to the heat, add the lightly beaten eggs, and cook to form a thin omelette. Carefully fold up the omelette and remove from the pan, then cut into 1cm slices. Return the oil to the pan and add the pork mixture. Stir-fry for about 5 minutes, then add the carrot and cook for about a minute longer.

Add the rice and second measure of oil, then stir in the shrimp and spring onion greens. Toss everything together, then stir-fry until the rice and shrimp are heated through. Sprinkle in the soy sauce and sugar and toss well.

Transfer to a serving dish and arrange the sliced cucumber around the edge, then top the rice with the sliced omelette and the fried spring onions.

*You can cook the rice the night before you intend to use it and store it in the fridge until required, or pop it in the microwave before heading off to work in the morning.

Spicy Mushroom Pilau

It may sound unusual, but this combination of flavours really is delicious!

For 3–4 servings:
1½ cups basmati rice
2 Tbsp canola oil
1 medium onion, diced
1–2 cloves garlic, chopped
2 tsp grated ginger
6 whole cloves
2 cardamom pods, crushed
2 bay leaves
½ tsp mustard seeds
½–1 tsp minced red chilli
250g mushrooms, sliced
½ red pepper, diced (optional)
2 cups hot water
2 tsp instant mushroom stock
2–3 Tbsp chopped coriander

Measure the rice into a large bowl and cover with cold water. Let it stand for 5–10 minutes.

Heat the oil in a large non-stick pan. Add the onion, garlic, ginger, spices and chilli. Cook, stirring frequently, until the onion is soft and turning clear. Add the mushrooms and red pepper (if using). Drain the rice, then add it to the pan along with the hot water and instant stock and stir until evenly mixed.

Allow the mixture to come to the boil, then reduce the heat to a very gentle simmer. Cover the pan with a close-fitting lid and cook for 10–15 minutes, until the rice is tender. Stir every few minutes to prevent sticking.

Season to taste with salt (if required), then stir in the fresh coriander and serve.

Spicy Indian Mince & Rice

This really simple meal has delicious Indian flavours.

For 4 servings:
2–3 Tbsp oil
1 large onion, diced
2 cloves garlic, chopped
1 Tbsp grated ginger
1 Tbsp curry powder
6–8 whole cloves
½ tsp cinnamon
2 bay leaves
3–4 cardamom pods, crushed (optional)
400–500g minced lamb
1 cup basmati rice
400g can whole tomatoes in juice
2 cups chicken stock
½ cup each slivered almonds and currants
1–2 Tbsp chopped coriander leaves

Heat the oil in a large pan (an electric frypan is ideal). Add the onion, garlic and ginger and cook, stirring frequently, until the onion begins to brown. Add the curry powder and spices and cook for 1–2 minutes longer, then stir in the mince.

Cook until the mince loses its pink colour, stirring frequently to break up any lumps. Add the rice, the tomatoes in juice and the stock. Break up the tomatoes and bring the mixture to the boil, then reduce the heat to a gentle simmer. Cover and cook, stirring occasionally, for about 15 minutes, or until the rice is tender.

Brown the almonds and 'puff up' the currants by heating them in a little oil in another frypan. Stir them into the mixture with the chopped coriander leaves. Cook for a minute or two longer before serving. Naan bread or poppadums make an ideal accompaniment.

Chicken Biryani

A biryani is a delicious layered rice and curry mixture – it does involve several steps, but all are simple and the results worthwhile.

For 3–4 servings:
1½ cups basmati rice
10cm cinnamon stick
4 cardamom pods, crushed
3 cups boiling water
2 Tbsp canola oil
1 medium onion, diced
2 cloves garlic, chopped
1–2 Tbsp grated ginger
300–400g boneless, skinless chicken
3 Tbsp Indian curry paste
400g can diced tomatoes in juice
1 tsp salt
1 cup peas
1–2 Tbsp each currants and sliced almonds

Place the rice, cinnamon stick and (flattened) cardamom pods in a large microwave bowl. Add the boiling water, cover, and microwave at Medium (50%) power for 15 minutes. (Do this in advance if you want.)

Heat the oil in a large non-stick pan, add the onion, garlic and ginger, and cook for about 5 minutes or until soft and beginning to brown. Add the chicken and stir-fry until no longer pink, then add curry paste. Cook, stirring frequently, for 1–2 minutes longer, then add the tomatoes and salt. Cook for another 2–3 minutes, then mix in the peas.

Spread half the rice over the bottom of a non-stick sprayed 20x30cm casserole dish. Spread the chicken mixture over the rice, then spread the remaining rice over this. Sprinkle the top with currants and sliced almonds, then cover with foil and bake at 180°C for 15–20 minutes. Serve with naan or other Indian breads, and a selection of chutneys.

Spinach & Rice Cake

Spinach, rice and eggs are baked together to form a substantial 'cake' – it's delicious served hot, warm or cold.

For 4 servings:
1 cup rice, brown or white
1 Tbsp oil
1 medium onion, diced
250g frozen spinach, thawed
½ tsp each basil & marjoram
1 tsp salt
black pepper to taste
1 cup (250g) cottage cheese
¼ cup grated Parmesan
3 large eggs
2–3 tomatoes, thinly sliced

Preheat the oven to 180°C. Bring a large pot of water to the boil and add the rice. Boil until the rice is just tender (8–10 minutes for white rice or 12–15 minutes for brown rice), then drain.

Heat the oil in a medium-sized pan. Add the onion and cook until the onion is soft and clear. Gently squeeze the spinach to get rid of excess water, then add it to the pan with the herbs, salt and pepper. Cook for 1–2 minutes, then transfer to a large bowl. Add the drained rice, cottage cheese, Parmesan, and eggs, and mix thoroughly.

Non-stick spray or oil a 22–25cm round cake tin and spoon in the rice mixture, smoothing off the top. Arrange the tomato slices over the surface, then bake at 180°C for 40 minutes. Serve with bread and a salad.

Baked Chicken on Spicy Rice Pilaf

I've been making this pilaf for years, but cooking the chicken on top is a new touch.

For 4 servings:
8 chicken drumsticks
½ tsp each cumin, cinnamon and chilli powder
2 small lemons
½ cup kalamata olives
3 Tbsp olive oil
1 medium onion, diced
2 cloves garlic, chopped
¼ cup pinenuts
¼ cup currants
½ tsp each cumin, coriander, cinnamon and chilli powder
1 cup long-grain rice
1 medium carrot, finely diced
zest of 1 lemon (optional)
3 cups boiling water
3 tsp instant chicken stock

Preheat the oven to 200°C. Place the chicken, spices, lemons (in thin wedges), olives and half the oil in a sturdy plastic bag. Massage bag so chicken is coated with the marinade. Set aside. Prepare the rice mixture.

Heat remaining oil in a flameproof casserole dish large enough to hold chicken pieces in a single layer. Add onion and garlic and cook until soft. Add pinenuts and currants and stir until nuts are golden brown. Add the spices, rice and carrot, lemon zest (if using), boiling water and instant stock.

Arrange chicken pieces, lemon wedges and olives on top, then bake for 30–40 minutes or until the chicken and rice are cooked. Serve with a simple green or tomato salad on the side.

Fragrant Coconut Rice with Fish

This dish is flavoured with Thai-inspired seasonings and is truly delicious.

For 2–3 servings:
2 stalks lemongrass
3 kaffir lime leaves
2 cloves garlic
1 tsp minced red chilli
1 cup coconut cream
1 Tbsp fish sauce
300–400g firm fish fillets (monkfish, snapper, groper, etc.)
2 Tbsp canola oil
1 medium onion, diced
1 Tbsp chopped ginger
1 cup Jasmine or basmati rice
2 cups boiling water
2 tsp instant chicken stock
½ red pepper, diced
½ cup frozen peas

Finely chop the tender parts of the lemongrass, lime leaves and garlic in a food processor. Add the chilli, coconut cream and fish sauce and process again.

Cut the fillets into 5–6cm chunky pieces and place in a small bowl. Add processed mixture and stir to coat. Set aside, then prepare the rice.

Cook the onion and ginger in the oil in a large, lidded, non-stick pan, until the onion is soft. Stir in the rice, then add the water, instant stock and the fish marinade (reserve the fish). Heat to boiling, then reduce the heat, cover and simmer gently for 10 minutes, stirring once or twice, until the rice is just tender. Stir in the vegetables and nestle the fish pieces into the rice. Cover the pan again and cook for a further 4–6 minutes until the thickest piece of fish is just cooked through.

Serve immediately, accompanied by a simple green or cucumber salad.

Paella

This recipe may stray a little from its Spanish roots, but it's still delicious!

For 2–3 large servings:
3 Tbsp olive oil
4 chicken wings or drumsticks
1 medium onion, diced
2–3 cloves of garlic
1 green and/or red pepper, sliced
¾ cup arborio or calrose rice
½ tsp each paprika and chilli powder
½ tsp turmeric or saffron
2 cups hot chicken stock
2 tomatoes, cubed
200g seafood (cubed fish fillets, cooked prawns, and/or sliced squid tubes)
4–6 live mussels
1 cup frozen peas or beans
2 Tbsp chopped parsley

Heat 1 tablespoon of oil in a large pan. Add the chicken pieces, brown on all sides, then remove from the pan. Add the remaining oil, onion and garlic, and cook until the onion has softened and slightly browned, stirring occasionally. Stir in the sliced pepper/s and cook for 1–2 minutes longer, then add the rice. Cook, stirring frequently, until the rice looks milky white.

Stir in the spices, stock and tomatoes, cover tightly, and bring to the boil. Simmer for about 15 minutes until the chicken and rice are cooked, stirring occasionally so the rice doesn't stick.

Add the seafood and the peas or beans. Stir, then top with the mussels. Replace the lid and cook until the mussels open and the fish is opaque, about 3–5 minutes. Sprinkle with parsley and serve immediately.

Spicy Gumbo

The first rule of gumbo is there are no rules… feel free to make substitutions or additions.

For 3–4 servings:
2 Tbsp canola oil
1 medium onion, diced
2 cloves garlic, chopped
100g ham, diced
2 chorizo sausages, sliced
1 red pepper, diced
2–3 sticks of celery, sliced
1 tsp paprika
½ tsp each chilli powder and thyme
2 bay leaves
400g can whole tomatoes in juice
1 cup chicken stock
1 cup corn kernels
2 cups cooked rice
1–2 cups cooked peeled shrimp, fresh or frozen (optional)
salt and pepper to taste
2–3 Tbsp chopped parsley

Heat the oil in a large non-stick pan or pot. Add the onion and garlic and cook, stirring frequently, until the onion is soft. Stir in the diced ham and sliced sausages and cook for about 3 minutes. Add the next six ingredients and cook, stirring continuously, for another 2–3 minutes.

Stir in the tomatoes in their juice (break up the whole tomatoes) and stock. Bring the mixture to the boil, then stir in the corn and cooked rice. Simmer until the corn is cooked, then add the shrimp (if using) and heat through.

Season to taste with salt (if required), then add the chopped parsley. Serve accompanied with crusty bread and/or a salad.

Ham & Tomato Risotto

This simple risotto is delicious any time but it's also a great way to use up any leftover Christmas ham.

For 2–3 servings:
2 Tbsp olive or canola oil
1 large onion, diced
1 clove garlic, chopped
250g ham, diced
1 cup arborio rice
2 cups chicken stock
½–1 cup hot water or dry white wine
3 medium tomatoes, diced
¼ cup grated Parmesan
¼ cup cream
¼ cup chopped fresh basil
salt and pepper to taste
additional basil and Parmesan to garnish

Heat the oil in a large pan. Add the onion and garlic and cook, without browning, until soft. Add the ham and cook until lightly browned. Tip in the rice and cook for 2–3 minutes longer, stirring constantly.

Pour in about ½ a cup of the stock, and stir constantly until the stock has almost disappeared, then add another ½ cup of liquid and repeat, stirring occasionally, until you have used about 2½ cups of liquid. When the risotto has cooked for about 20 minutes (if the mixture looks too dry add the extra ½ cup of liquid) and the rice is just cooked through, add the tomatoes, Parmesan, cream and basil. Stir to combine and season to taste with salt and pepper.

Heat through, then serve immediately, garnished with a few basil leaves. Accompany with some crusty bread and a crisp green salad.

Chicken & Mushroom Risotto

This can be put together in less than 40 minutes – with very little forethought or planning.

For 2–3 servings:
2 Tbsp olive or canola oil
1 medium onion, diced
2 cloves garlic, chopped
250–300g cubed chicken
250g mushrooms, sliced
½ red pepper, diced
1 tsp thyme
1 cup arborio rice
2½ cups boiling water
2 tsp instant mushroom stock
¼ cup cream
½ cup grated Parmesan
salt and pepper to taste
basil or thyme and a little additional Parmesan to garnish

Heat the oil in a large non-stick pan. Add the onion and garlic and cook, stirring frequently, until soft. Add the chicken and cook until it is no longer pink. Stir in the mushrooms, red pepper and thyme and cook, stirring occasionally, until the mushrooms soften. Add the rice and cook for 2–3 minutes longer.

Add 1 cup of water and the instant stock powder. Bring to the boil, then reduce the heat and cook, stirring frequently, until the liquid has almost disappeared. Add the remaining water half a cup at a time, simmering and stirring frequently until the liquid has almost gone before making the next addition. After about 20 minutes, test to see if the rice is cooked. Add another ¼–½ cup water and simmer for a few minutes longer if necessary. Add the cream and Parmesan, and season to taste with salt and pepper.

Heat through, then serve immediately, garnished with a little basil or thyme and grated Parmesan. A crisp green salad, some crusty bread and a glass of wine make ideal accompaniments.

Pumpkin & Mushroom Risotto

The sweetness of pumpkin and the earthiness of mushrooms combine perfectly to give this risotto a wonderful flavour.

For 3–4 large servings:
1 medium onion
2 Tbsp olive or canola oil
1 clove garlic, chopped
250g peeled pumpkin
250g Swiss brown mushrooms
1 Tbsp olive or canola oil
1 cup arborio rice
2½–3 cups hot water or mushroom stock
1 Tbsp basil pesto
2–3 Tbsp grated Parmesan cheese
½–1 cup fresh or frozen peas
½–1 tsp salt
black pepper to taste

Peel, quarter and slice the onion while the oil heats in a large (preferably non-stick) frypan. Add the onion and garlic and cook for 2–3 minutes until the onion is softening. Grate the pumpkin and halve the mushrooms, then add these and continue to cook, stirring frequently to avoid browning, for about 5 minutes. Remove the vegetable mixture from the pan and set aside.

Heat the second measure of oil in the pan, then stir in the rice and cook for 1–2 minutes. Add the vegetable mixture and stir gently, then pour in 1 cup of the water or stock. Bring to the boil, then reduce the heat and leave the uncovered pan to simmer gently, stirring occasionally, until most of the liquid has disappeared (this should take 3–4 minutes). Add another cup of liquid and when this liquid too has been absorbed (in another 4–5 minutes), add another ½ cup of liquid and leave to simmer again.

When this liquid has almost gone, test the rice to see if it is done. If the liquid has all gone before the rice is cooked, gradually add an extra half cup or so. Test the rice frequently, taking care not to overcook it or it will turn mushy – but do not serve undercooked either, as hard-centred rice is very unpleasant!

As soon as the grains are tender right through, add the pesto, Parmesan and peas. Stir frequently for another 3–4 minutes until the peas are cooked. Season to taste and serve immediately. (You may not need any salt if you used instant stock.)

Noodles

Peanutty Noodle Salad

This salad makes a delicious meal on its own, but if you want something more substantial, add a little cooked or smoked chicken.

For 4–6 servings:
3 Tbsp peanut butter
2 tsp sesame oil
1 Tbsp each sherry and brown sugar
2 Tbsp each light soy sauce and canola oil
1 clove garlic, minced
2 Tbsp grated fresh ginger
¼ cup hot water
2–3 Tbsp chopped fresh coriander leaf
½–1 tsp minced red chilli
salt to taste

250g fine or ribbon egg noodles
1 large carrot
½ cup whole green beans
½ small cucumber
1–2 spring onions
2 Tbsp lime or lemon juice
chopped fresh chilli (optional)

Prepare the dressing by measuring the first 11 ingredients into a screw-top jar and shaking until well combined. Add the salt to taste, then leave to stand while you prepare the remaining ingredients.

Cook the noodles until they are just done (over-cooked noodles will be soggy and weak). Drain, then rinse them well with cold water. Toss the noodles with a little oil and set aside. Cut the carrot into fine strips or matchsticks, and combine these with the beans in a shallow pan. Cover with water and boil for about 1 minute. Drain and set aside with the noodles.

Halve the cucumber lengthways and scoop out and discard the seeds, then cut as you did the carrot. Cut the white section of the spring onion/s lengthwise into fine strips (keep some of the green part for a garnish), and add these to the other vegetables.

Toss the noodles, vegetables and dressing together in a large bowl. If possible leave to stand for 15–30 minutes, then sprinkle with the lime or lemon juice and toss again. Garnish with some chopped spring onion greens and/or fresh red chilli and serve.

Crispy Noodle Salad

Tender, moist chicken breast is offset by crisp vegetables, crunchy noodles, and a distinctly Asian flavoured dressing.

For 4 main servings:

400g boneless, skinless chicken breasts
1 Tbsp light soy sauce
1 Tbsp sesame oil
1 Tbsp cornflour
2 Tbsp sugar
1 tsp instant chicken stock
¼ cup water
¼ cup rice or wine vinegar
¼ cup light soy sauce
1 Tbsp sesame oil
1 Tbsp grated ginger
1 large clove garlic, chopped
1 medium iceberg lettuce
1 avocado, cubed
1–2 medium carrots, cut into matchsticks
½ small cucumber, julienned
½–1 cup daikon matchsticks
200–250g crispy noodles*

Marinate the chicken breasts in the soy and sesame oil for at least 30 minutes, preferably longer.

To make the dressing, combine the cornflour, sugar, instant stock and water in a small pot. Heat until boiling, stirring frequently, then remove from the heat and add the next five ingredients. (This will make about 1 cup of dressing, enough for two of these salads; keep the extra in the fridge in an airtight container for up to 10 days.)

Grill or fry the chicken, then slice into strips about 1cm wide.

To assemble the salad, tear the lettuce into bite-sized pieces. Toss it together with the other prepared vegetables, the crispy noodles and the warm chicken strips.

Pour the dressing over the salad just before serving, or serve it separately for your diners to add themselves.

*Crispy noodles are curly, yellow, fried wheat or egg noodles, about 4mm thick – not fried rice or bean thread noodles. They are available pre-cooked in Asian food stores and some supermarkets.

Thai-Style Chicken & Noodle Salad

This Thai-style salad is quick to prepare and makes a great meal on a warm evening.

For 3–4 servings:
250–300g fine egg noodles
3 Tbsp canola oil
2 cloves garlic, chopped
1–2 Tbsp grated ginger
450g minced chicken
1 tsp Thai red curry paste
1 tsp minced red chilli
¼ cup basil leaves
1 Tbsp fish sauce
1 Tbsp light soy sauce
1 tsp sugar
juice 2 lemons
4 cups (about 100g) mesclun
¼ cup chopped peanuts to garnish

Cook the noodles in plenty of lightly salted boiling water. Rinse with plenty of cold water, then drain well and return to the cooking pot. Add 1 tablespoon of the oil and toss gently to coat.

Heat the remaining oil in a large pan. Add the garlic and ginger and cook for about 1 minute, then add the chicken, curry paste and chilli. Cook, stirring frequently to break up any large lumps, for about 5 minutes or until lightly browned.

Stir in the basil leaves, fish and soy sauces, sugar, and the juice of one of the lemons, and cook for a further 2–3 minutes, stirring occasionally, then remove from the heat.

Scatter the mesclun over a large platter, arrange the noodles over this, then top with the chicken. Sprinkle with the juice of the second lemon and the peanuts, then serve.

Chilled Soba Noodle Salad

Soba noodles originate in Japan. Unlike most pasta, they are made from buckwheat rather than conventional flour, which gives them a slightly nutty flavour.

For 2–3 servings:
250g soba noodles
½ small cucumber, deseeded
1 medium carrot
¼ small daikon* (optional)
2 Tbsp lime or lemon juice
2 Tbsp light soy sauce
3–4 Tbsp peanut oil
1–2 tsp finely grated fresh ginger
1 Tbsp canola oil
2 tsp dark sesame oil
1–2 Tbsp toasted sesame seeds

* Daikon is a large, mild white radish.

Put the noodles on to cook in plenty of boiling water. While they cook, cut the cucumber, carrot and daikon into long, thin matchsticks. Soften the carrot sticks by plunging them briefly into boiling water. Prepare the dressing by combining the lime or lemon juice with the soy sauce, oil and grated ginger.

Rinse cooked noodles with plenty of cold water. Toss the cooked noodles with the canola and sesame oils. Tip the noodles and vegetables into a large bowl. Add the dressing and half of the sesame seeds and toss together.

Sprinkle with the remaining sesame seeds and serve immediately or refrigerate until required.

Summer Rolls

These simple and delicious rolls (cousins of the more familiar spring rolls) are wrapped in soft rice paper and served as is rather than fried.

For 3–4 servings:
½ cup water
¼ cup light soy sauce
2 Tbsp brown sugar
2 Tbsp sherry
2 cloves garlic, chopped
1 Tbsp grated ginger
½ tsp five spice powder
300–400g boneless, skinless chicken breasts
12–16 rice paper wrappers

Dipping Sauce: Combine the juice of 1 lime, ¼ cup water, ¼ cup fish sauce, 1 Tbsp caster sugar, 2 cloves finely chopped garlic and about 1 tsp finely chopped red chilli in a small bowl and leave to stand for at least 5 minutes.

Mix the first seven ingredients in a frypan, then add the chicken and simmer gently, turning once or twice, for about 15 minutes, or until the chicken is cooked. Remove from the heat and leave to cool in the cooking liquid.

Prepare dipping sauce (see recipe on the left). Gather together extra fillings for the rolls. My favourites are chopped mint leaves and/or coriander leaves, soaked glass noodles or fine rice sticks, bean sprouts, finely shredded lettuce, grated carrot, chopped peanuts and chives.

Shred the chicken, place it in a small bowl, and toss with 1–2 tablespoons of cooking liquid.

To make a roll, soak a wrapper in warm water until soft and white. Place some chicken and your choice of extras on the wrapper. Fold in the edges and roll up to make a little parcel. Dip into the sauce and enjoy!

Tom Yum Plus

Chilli and lime give this simple Thai classic a wonderful hot and sour flavour.

For 2–3 servings:
250g (about 12) raw prawns
4 cups water
2cm fresh ginger, chopped
1 stalk lemongrass, halved
3–4 kaffir lime leaves*
½–1 tsp minced red chilli
1 stalk lemongrass, finely sliced
3–4 Tbsp lime juice
50–100g rice noodles
250g button mushrooms
1 medium carrot, julienned
250g firm fish, cubed
2–3 Tbsp fish sauce, to taste
2 Tbsp chopped coriander
1 spring onion, sliced
sliced red chilli and additional
   coriander to garnish

* *Kaffir lime leaves are available fresh in larger supermarkets or dried from stores specialising in Asian foods.*

To prepare the stock, remove the tails from the prawns and set aside. Place the heads in a large pot with the water, ginger, first stalk of lemongrass, and the lime leaves. Bring to the boil and simmer for about 10 minutes. While the stock simmers, peel and de-vein the prawn tails (add the shells to the stock).

Strain the stock into a clean pot (return the lime leaves to the stock), then add the next six ingredients (vary the amount of chilli to taste). Simmer gently for about three minutes until the noodles and vegetables are cooked, then add the prawn tails and cubed fish. Simmer for 1–2 minutes longer, or until the fish has turned white and is just cooked through. Remove from the heat, then add fish sauce to taste and the chopped coriander and spring onion.

Divide soup between serving bowls and garnish with some thinly sliced red chilli and a few coriander leaves and serve immediately.

Salmon, Spinach & Udon Soup

You won't believe how good a bowl of soup made this quickly can be!

For 3–4 servings:
300–400g salmon fillet
1 clove garlic, chopped
2 Tbsp ginger, chopped
3 Tbsp Kikkoman soy sauce
2 tsp sesame oil
410g can chicken consommé
2–3 cups water
100g mushrooms, sliced
1 red pepper, sliced
200g spinach leaves
400g udon noodles
salt and pepper to taste

Skin and bone the salmon if necessary, then cut into 1.5cm cubes. Place in a shallow container with the garlic, 1 tablespoon each of the ginger and soy sauce, and 1 teaspoon of the sesame oil. Stir gently to combine and set aside.

Pour the consommé and water into a large pot, add the remaining ginger, soy sauce and sesame oil, and stir to combine. Stir in the mushrooms and red pepper and then heat to boiling. Drop in the spinach and the noodles and allow to return to the boil.

Tip in the salmon cubes and stir gently to combine. Simmer the soup for 2–3 minutes longer until the salmon is just cooked through, then season to taste with salt and pepper. Ladle into bowls and serve.

Seafood Laksa

This is my all time favourite soup. Try it like this or replace the fish with cooked chicken instead.

For 3–4 servings:
2 Tbsp curry powder
2–3 Tbsp cashew nuts
2–3cm fresh ginger, peeled
2 cloves garlic, peeled
2–3 Tbsp chopped lemongrass, or zest of 1 lime
1–2 tsp Thai red curry paste
2 Tbsp each light soy sauce and water
2 Tbsp canola oil
400ml can coconut cream
3 cups chicken stock
400–500g fresh egg noodles*
400–500g firm fish fillets, cut in 2–3cm cubes
1 medium-large carrot, julienned
100g spinach leaves or green beans
100–200g cooked prawns (optional)
100–200g bean sprouts
chopped fresh coriander and/or spring onion to garnish

Combine the first eight ingredients in a blender or food processor (or mortar and pestle) and process to make a smooth paste. The Thai curry paste is not absolutely necessary, but it adds to the 'depth' of flavour.

Heat the oil in a large pot, then add the paste and cook, stirring continuously, for 1 minute. Add the coconut cream and stock (or water plus instant stock). Bring the soup to the boil and add the noodles, fish, carrot and green vegetables and simmer for 2–3 minutes until the cubes of fish are just cooked through. During this time divide the prawns and bean sprouts between the serving bowls.

Ladle the soup into the bowls, dividing the fish etc. evenly between each. Garnish with a few extra bean sprouts and some chopped coriander and/or sliced spring onion and serve immediately.

*Fresh egg noodles can be replaced with rice sticks if required. Soak 250g thick rice sticks in boiling water for 5–10 minutes, then divide them between the bowls with the prawns and sprouts rather than simmering them in the soup.

Pho Ga (Vietnamese Chicken Soup)

I think assembling food at the table is fun, and this simple soup is no exception.

For 4 servings:
3–4 cups chicken stock (see recipe)
2 Tbsp fish sauce
½ tsp each of salt and sugar
250g wide rice (cellophane) noodles, soaked in hot water for 15–20 minutes, then drained
300–400g cooked chicken meat, shredded
1 medium carrot, julienned
100–150g bean sprouts
6–8 mushrooms, sliced
3 spring onions, finely sliced
2 sticks celery, finely sliced
2 hard-boiled eggs (optional)
coriander leaf, whole or chopped
chilli flakes or chopped fresh chilli
hoisin sauce (optional)

Prepare the chicken stock as described below, then add the fish sauce, salt and sugar. Taste and add a little more of any of these if you think necessary. While the stock heats until almost boiling, prepare the remaining ingredients, placing each in a separate bowl. Transfer the heated broth to a serving bowl and arrange the bowls of prepared ingredients around this.

The soup should be served in deep bowls and is assembled as follows: place a handful of noodles in the bottom of the bowl, and top with some shredded chicken, some strands of carrot, some sprouts, a few sliced mushrooms, chopped spring onions, celery, chopped egg (if using), and coriander leaf. Ladle in some of the hot broth, then finish by topping with a little chilli and some hoisin sauce if desired. Enjoy!

Chicken Stock

2–3 chicken breasts or legs (about 600g)
1 small onion, quartered
1 small carrot, quartered
4 cups water
1cm piece ginger root, halved
5cm cinnamon stick
a few black pepper corns

Place all the stock ingredients in a pot and bring to the boil. Reduce the heat and simmer for about 20 minutes. Remove the chicken pieces from the stock and separate the meat from the skin and bones. Shred the meat and set it aside for use in the soup, then return the skin and bones to the stock and simmer for another 30 minutes or so. Strain the stock and 'assemble' your soup.

VARIATION: Instead of making stock, combine a 420g can of chicken consommé or broth with 1½ cups water and the quantities of ginger, cinnamon stick and pepper corns used above. Heat until boiling, then strain. Use any cold shredded chicken, or cooked sliced steak, etc.

Curried Chicken & Noodle Stir-fry

This delicious recipe originated as an attempt to emulate a favourite noodle dish of mine, bami goreng.

For 2–3 servings:
2 Tbsp canola oil
1 medium onion, sliced
2–3 cloves garlic, chopped
350g boneless, skinless chicken
1 Tbsp curry powder
1 large carrot, julienned
1–2 cups broccoli florets
2 spring onions, sliced
400–500g fresh egg noodles*
½ cup hot water
2 Tbsp soy sauce
½ tsp each salt and sugar
3–4 Tbsp chopped coriander

*If you can't find fresh noodles, cook 200g fine egg noodles and use these instead.

Prepare all the ingredients, then heat the oil in a wok or very large pan. Add the onion and garlic and stir-fry until the onion begins to soften. Stir in the chicken and continue to cook, stirring frequently, until the chicken is no longer pink. Add the curry powder and stir-fry for about a minute longer.

Add the vegetables and stir-fry for 1–2 minutes. Tease the noodles apart and add them to the pan. Tip in the water, soy sauce, salt and sugar. Toss together until well combined, then cook for about 2 minutes (covering the wok/pan if you have a lid big enough). Toss again and cook 2 minutes more. Add an extra ¼ cup of water and cook for 2 minutes longer if the noodles are not tender.

Divide into serving bowls or plates, sprinkle with the chopped coriander, and serve immediately.

Honey-Soy Chicken & Noodles

Both the chicken and noodles are delicious in this sweet and tangy glaze.

For 3–4 servings:
200g fine egg noodles
3 Tbsp canola oil
2 tsp cornflour
½ cup cold water
3 Tbsp honey
2 Tbsp soy sauce
2 Tbsp lemon juice
1 medium onion
2 cloves garlic, chopped
1 Tbsp grated ginger
300–350g boneless, skinless chicken, thinly sliced
1 medium carrot, julienned
½ red pepper, sliced
2 baby bok choy, quartered
1 tsp sesame oil

Cook the noodles according to the instructions on the packet, then rinse and drain them. Return noodles to the cooking pot, add 1 tablespoon of oil and toss to coat, then set aside.

Measure the cornflour into a small bowl. Add the water, honey, soy sauce and lemon juice and stir to combine.

Heat the remaining oil in a large pan or wok over a high heat. Add the onion, garlic and ginger and stir-fry for 1–2 minutes, then add the chicken. Continue to cook, stirring frequently until the chicken is lightly browned.

Add the remaining vegetables and stir-fry for 1–2 minutes longer, then add the noodles and stir/toss to combine. Stir the sauce (cornflour tends to settle), then pour it over the noodle mixture. Cook for 2–3 minutes longer until the sauce thickens to make a shiny glaze. Sprinkle with the sesame oil and serve.

Pad Thai (Thai-style Fried Noodles)

These tasty stir-fried noodles can be prepared in about fifteen minutes from start to finish.

For 2–3 servings:
150–200g rice noodles
1 Tbsp canola oil
1 large egg, lightly beaten
3 cloves garlic, crushed, peeled and chopped
2 (about 200g total) boneless, skinless chicken breasts, thinly sliced
1 tsp minced red chilli
200g cooked shrimp, thawed and drained if frozen
1 Tbsp canola oil
4 spring onions, sliced diagonally
3 Tbsp fish sauce
2 Tbsp rice (or wine) vinegar
1 Tbsp lime (or lemon) juice
2 Tbsp sugar
1–2 cups bean sprouts
chopped fresh coriander and roasted peanuts to garnish

Place the rice noodles in a large bowl, cover with boiling water and soak for 5–10 minutes or until soft and flexible, then drain well. (Check after five minutes as different brands seem to soften at different speeds and some get too soft if soaked for too long.)

Heat about 1 teaspoon of the oil in a large wok or frypan, then add the beaten egg and cook to form a thin omelette. As soon as the upper surface looks dry, roll or fold the omelette and remove it from the pan. Cut it into 1cm ribbons and set aside.

Add the rest of the first measure of oil to the pan, then add the garlic and cook over a high heat until it begins to brown. Add the chicken and stir-fry for 3–4 minutes until it has lost its pink colour and is beginning to brown.

Stir in the chilli and shrimp and stir-fry for a minute longer, then add the noodles, second measure of oil and the spring onion greens. Toss to combine, then add the fish sauce, vinegar, lime (or lemon) juice and sugar.

Stir-fry until the liquid has almost disappeared, then add the bean sprouts and cook for 1 minute longer.

Serve immediately, garnished with chopped coriander and peanuts.

Sweet Chilli Salmon on Sesame Noodles

Moist glazed salmon on a bed of tasty noodles makes a fantastic easy meal.

For 2 servings:
300g salmon fillet
¼ cup sweet chilli sauce
3–4 Tbsp chopped coriander
1 Tbsp lemon juice
1 Tbsp Kikkoman soy sauce
2 tsp sesame oil
200g Asian egg noodles or vermicelli
1 medium carrot, julienned
10–15cm telegraph cucumber, julienned
100g daikon, julienned (optional)
1 Tbsp canola oil
1 Tbsp sesame oil
1 Tbsp Kikkoman soy sauce
1 tsp grated ginger
½ tsp salt
1 tsp toasted sesame seeds

Cut the salmon into serving-sized pieces, then place in a plastic bag and add the next five ingredients. Massage the bag so the salmon is coated, then set aside. Turn the grill on to preheat, placing a grill tray 7–10cm below the element.

Meanwhile, bring a large pot of lightly salted water to the boil. Add the noodles and cook until tender (the time will vary according to the type of noodle you use). While the noodles cook, prepare the vegetables. When the noodles are cooked, drain them well and rinse briefly with cold water. Return the noodles to the cooking pot, add the remaining ingredients, and toss to mix.

Arrange the marinated salmon pieces, skin side down, on a double layer of foil, and (carefully) place this on the heated grill tray (this helps the skin side cook). Grill the salmon 7–10cm from the heat for 3–5 minutes depending on thickness.

Place the cooked salmon on a nest of the warm sesame-noodle mixture and serve immediately.

Black Bean Beef & Noodles

The salty pungency of black beans always goes particularly well with beef, and this is no exception.

For 3–4 servings:
2 Tbsp canola oil
1 medium onion, diced
2 Tbsp grated ginger
400g lean minced beef
2 Tbsp black bean and garlic sauce*
1 medium carrot, julienned
1 green pepper, sliced
2 Tbsp sherry
2 Tbsp light soy sauce
400–500g fresh egg noodles
½ cup water
chopped coriander or spring onion to garnish

* This sauce is available in jars at larger supermarkets.

Heat the oil in a very large frypan or wok. Add the onion and ginger, and cook until the onion begins to soften. Add the beef and cook, stirring frequently to break up any lumps, until it has lost its pink colour. Stir in the black bean sauce.

Add the carrot, green pepper, sherry, and soy sauce, and stir-fry until the vegetables have softened.

Place the noodles in a large sieve or colander and rinse them with very hot or boiling water. Drain them and add to the beef mixture. Stir gently to combine, then add the water. Cook, stirring occasionally, for 3–4 minutes or until most of the liquid is absorbed.

Serve garnished with chopped coriander or thinly sliced spring onions.

Fresh Noodles with Five-Spice Chicken

Just the thought of tender pieces of chicken marinated and cooked in this fragrant five spice mixture has my mouth watering.

For 3–4 servings:
400g boneless, skinless chicken
2 Tbsp each light soy sauce and sherry
2 tsp sesame oil
½ tsp five spice powder
3 Tbsp canola oil
2 cloves garlic, chopped
3 spring onions, sliced
1 large carrot, julienned
1 medium red pepper, sliced
400–500g fresh egg noodles
½ cup water
2 Tbsp light soy sauce
2 Tbsp hoisin sauce
2 cups thinly sliced cabbage
2–3 Tbsp chopped coriander
extra ¼ cup water if required

Cut the chicken into bite-sized cubes or slices and combine with next four ingredients. Cover and leave to marinate for at least half an hour.

Heat the oil in a large wok or pan, add the chicken and garlic, and stir-fry over a high heat until the chicken is lightly browned on all sides. Add the spring onions, carrot, red pepper and fresh noodles. Reduce the heat, then add the water and the soy and hoisin sauces. Toss everything together, then cover and leave to simmer for 5 minutes, stirring once or twice.

Stir in the chopped cabbage and coriander leaf, plus the additional water if the mixture looks too dry (it should have a nice moist gleam, but not be swimming in liquid). Cover and cook for another 2 minutes. Serve immediately.

Index

30 minute Bolognese	14
Alison's lazy lasagne	27
almond, broccoli & mushroom pasta sauce	12
Bacon & egg pasta	20
bacon & mushroom sauce, pasta with	18
baked chicken on spicy rice pilaf	39
basic beef lasagne	23
basil pesto	8
beef lasagne, basic	23
beef, black bean & noodles	62
biryani, chicken	38
black bean beef & noodles	62
Bolognese, 30 minute	14
broccoli, mushroom & almond pasta sauce	12
Cajun rice gumbo	40
cake, spinach & rice	38
cannelloni, salmon & mushroom	28
cheese, macaroni	14
chicken & crispy noodle salad	48
chicken & mushroom risotto	42
chicken & noodle salad, Thai-style	50
chicken & noodles, honey-soy	57
chicken baked on spicy pilaf	39
chicken biryani	38
chicken fried rice	34
chicken soup, Vietnamese	56
chicken, five spice with fresh noodles	62
chicken, Vietnamese rice paper rolls	51
chilled soba noodle salad	51
coconut rice with fish	39
crispy noodle salad	48
curried chicken & noodle stir-fry	57
Easy spaghetti & meatballs	22
egg & bacon pasta sauce	20
Fettuccine with ham & peas	20
fish with fragrant coconut rice	39
five spice chicken with noodles	62
fragrant coconut rice with fish	39
fresh noodles with five-spice chicken	62
fried noodles, Thai-style	58
fried rice, chicken	34
fried rice, Indonesian nasi goreng	35
Gumbo, spicy	40
Ham & peas, fettuccine with	20
ham & tomato risotto	42
hand rolls, sushi	31
honey-soy chicken & noodles	57
Indian mince & rice, spicy	36
Indonesian fried rice, nasi goreng	35
Laksa, curried seafood noodle soup	54
lasagne, Alison's lazy	27
lasagne, basic beef	23
lasagne, smoked salmon & mushroom	26
lasagne, spinach & mushroom	24
lazy lasagne	27
Macaroni cheese	14
meatballs, spaghetti with	22
mince & rice, spicy Indian	36
minestrone	7
moulded sushi	31
mushroom & bacon sauce, pasta with	18
mushroom & chicken risotto	42
mushroom & pumpkin risotto	44
mushroom & salmon cannelloni	28
mushroom & spinach lasagne	24
mushroom, broccoli & almond pasta sauce	12
mussels & spaghetti	16
Nasi goreng, Indonesian fried rice	35
Nicoise, pasta salad	10
noodle salad, crispy	48
noodle salad, peanutty	47
noodle salad, Thai-style chicken	50
noodle soup, curried seafood laksa	54
noodle soup, udon with salmon & spinach	52
noodle, curried chicken stir-fry	57
noodles, black bean beef &	62
noodles, fresh with five-spice chicken	62
noodles, honey-soy chicken	57
noodles, sesame with sweet chilli salmon	60
noodles, Thai-style fried	58
Pad Thai (Thai-style fried noodles)	58
paella	40
pasta & bean soup	8
pasta Nicoise	10
pasta primavera	12
pasta with bacon & egg sauce	20
pasta with bacon & mushroom sauce	18
pasta with broccoli, mushroom & almonds	12
pasta with pistachio & parsley pesto	10
peanutty noodle salad	47
peas & ham, fettuccine with	20
penne with broccoli, mushroom & almonds	12
pesto, basil	8
pesto, pistachio & parsley	10
pho ga (Vietnamese chicken soup)	56
pilaf, chicken baked on	39
pilau, spicy rice	36
pistachio & parsley pesto	10
primavera sauce	12
pumpkin & mushroom risotto	44
puttanesca sauce, spaghetti with	16
Rice & spinach cake	38
rice paper rolls	51
rice pilaf, chicken baked on	39
rice with chicken and seafood, paella	40
rice, baked chicken biryani	38
rice, fragrant coconut with fish	39
rice, fried chicken	34
rice, gumbo	40
rice, spicy pilau	36
risotto, chicken & mushroom	42
risotto, ham & tomato	42
risotto, pumpkin & mushroom	44
rolled sushi	31
rolls, Vietnamese rice paper	51
Salad pasta & tuna	10
salad, chilled soba noodle	51
salad, crispy noodle & chicken	48
salad, pasta Nicoise	10
salad, peanutty noodle	47
salad, sushi rice	32
salad, Thai-style chicken & noodle	50
salmon & mushroom cannelloni	28
salmon, smoked & mushroom lasagne	26
salmon, spinach & udon soup	52
salmon, sweet chilli on sesame noodles	60
seafood and chicken paella	40
seafood laksa	54
seafood soup, tom yum	52
sesame noodle with sweet chilli salmon	60
smoked salmon & mushroom lasagne	26
soba noodle salad, chilled	51
soup, pasta & bean	8
soup, pasta & vegetable	7
soup, seafood laksa	54
soup, Thai-style seafood, tom yum	52
soup, udon with spinach & salmon	52
soup, vegetable & pasta	7
soup, Vietnamese chicken pho ga	56
spaghetti & meatballs, easy	22
spaghetti & mussels	16
spaghetti Bolognese	14
spaghetti puttanesca	16
spicy gumbo	40
spicy Indian mince & rice	36
spicy rice pilau	36
spicy tomato sauce, puttanesca	16
spinach & mushroom lasagne	24
spinach & rice cake	38
stir-fry, curried chicken & noodle	57
stock, Asian chicken	56
summer rolls	51
sushi	31
sushi rice salad	32
sweet chilli salmon on sesame noodles	60
Thai-style chicken & noodle salad	50
Thai-style fried noodles, pad Thai	58
Thai-style seafood soup, tom yum	52
tom yum plus (Thai-style seafood soup)	52
tomato sauce, spicy	16
Udon noodle soup, spinach & salmon	52
Vietnamese chicken soup	56
Vietnamese rice paper rolls	51

Knives by Mail Order

For about 20 years Alison has imported her favourite, very sharp kitchen knives from Switzerland. They keep their edges well, are easy to sharpen, a pleasure to use, and make excellent gifts.

VEGETABLE KNIFE $8.00
Ideal for cutting and peeling vegetables, these knives have a straight edged 85mm blade and black (dishwasher-proof) nylon handle. Each knife comes in an individual plastic sheath.

BONING/UTILITY KNIFE $9.50
Excellent for boning chicken and other meats, and/or for general kitchen duties. Featuring a 103mm blade that curves to a point and a dishwasher-proof, black nylon handle. Each knife comes in a plastic sheath.

SERRATED KNIFE $9.50
These knives are unbelievably useful. They are perfect for cutting cooked meats, ripe fruit and vegetables, and slicing bread and baking. Treated carefully, these blades stay sharp for years. The serrated 110mm blade is rounded at the end with a black (dishwasher-proof) nylon handle and each knife comes in an individual plastic sheath.

THREE-PIECE SET $22.00
This three-piece set includes a vegetable knife, a serrated knife (as described above) and a right-handed potato peeler with a matching black handle, presented in a white plastic wallet.

GIFT BOXED KNIFE SET $44.00
This set contains five knives plus a matching right-handed potato peeler. There is a straight bladed vegetable knife and a serrated knife (as above), as well as a handy 85mm serrated blade vegetable knife, a small (85mm) utility knife with a pointed tip and a smaller (85mm) serrated knife. These elegantly presented sets make ideal gifts.

SERRATED CARVING KNIFE $28.50
This fabulous knife cuts beautifully and is a pleasure to use; it's ideal for carving or cutting fresh bread. The 21cm serrated blade does not require sharpening. Once again the knife has a black moulded, dishwasher safe handle and comes in a plastic sheath.

COOK'S KNIFE $35.00
An excellent all-purpose kitchen knife. With a well balanced 19cm wedge-shaped blade and a contoured black nylon handle, these knives make short work of slicing and chopping, and have come out on top of their class in several comparative tests. Each dishwasher-safe knife comes with its own plastic sheath.

VICTORNOX MULTIPURPOSE KITCHEN SHEARS $29.50
Every kitchen should have a pair of these! With their comfortable nylon handles and sharp blades these quality shears make short work of everything from cutting a piece of string or sheet of paper to jointing a whole chicken. Note: Black handle only.

STEEL $20.00
These steels have a 20cm 'blade' and measure 33cm in total. With its matching black handle the steel is an ideal companion for your own knives, or as a gift. Alison gets excellent results using these steels. N.B. Not for use with serrated knives.

PROBUS SPREADER/SCRAPER $7.50
After her knives, these are the most used tools in Alison's kitchen! With a comfortable plastic handle, metal shank and flexible plastic blade (suitable for use on non-stick surfaces), these are excellent for mixing muffin batters, stirring and scraping bowls, spreading icings, turning pikelets etc., etc…

NON-STICK LINERS
Re-usable SureBrand PTFE non-stick liners are another essential kitchen item – they really help avoid the frustration of stuck-on baking, roasting or frying. Once you've used them, you'll wonder how you did without!

Round tin liner	(for 15-23cm tins)	$6.50
	(for 23-30cm tins)	$9.50
Square tin liner	(for 15-23cm tins)	$6.50
	(for 23-30cm tins)	$9.50
Ring tin liner	(for 23cm tins)	$6.95
Baking sheet liner	(33x44cm)	$13.95
Barbeque Liner	(Heavy duty 33x44cm)	$17.95
Frypan Liner	(Heavy duty round 30cm)	$10.95

All prices include GST. Prices current at time of publishing, subject to change without notice. Please add $5.00 post & packing to any order (any number of items).

Make cheques payable to Alison Holst Mail Orders and post to:

Alison Holst Mail Orders
FREEPOST 124807
PO Box 17016
Wellington

or visit: **www.holst.co.nz**